FRAGMENTS

FRAGMENTS

ISBN (paperback): 978-1-968919-37-5
ISBN (ebook): 978-1-968919-38-2

Armin Lear Press, Inc.
215 W Riverside Drive, #4362
Estes Park, CO 80517

FRAGMENTS

A memory play

JIM PETOSA

In loving memory of my life-partner,
Raymond Luis Davila (1953–1990) and my husband,
Jamie Shawn Grassmann (1964–2025).

You are remembered every day.

"Death destroys a man,
but the idea of death saves him."
E. M. Forster

ACKNOWLEDGMENTS

To all the friends and family who listened to these stories through the years and encouraged me to write them down, thank you.

Among them are the following who contributed in many ways and to varying degrees. I am indebted to each. Bill Chisholm, Maryann Karinch, Brenda Reed, Lockwood Brown, Clay Hopper, James Noone, Jon Adler, Jenn Beatty, Barbara Pinolini, Paula Langton and Ken Cheeseman, and the good people of the Becket Arts Center in Becket, Massachusetts, Jim Frangione and Judy Braha of the Great Barrington Public Theatre, the congregation of United First Parish Church (Unitarian Universalist) in Quincy, Massachusetts, and the extraordinary community of men who gather at the Rowe UU Camp and Conference Center in Rowe, Massachusetts.

PREFACE

This memoir is written as a series of episodes. I call them fragments. Each one seems mystically selected because they are indelibly etched in my brain. That is how memory works. The story begins in 1985 and ends in 1990. There are ten fragments and an epilogue. For many years, I shared these fragments as oral histories to friends who had the patience and the interest to hear them. Over time, each fragment developed distinct characteristics, with an attention to specific details, and a recollection of how particular phrases were spoken. All the events in this memoir are true to my recollection. Every spoken word recorded here is either exact or as accurate as my memory permits.

This memoir exists because, as time goes by, our shared memories of the era and circumstances surrounding this journey gradually diminish. We must ensure these stories are preserved by documenting them and sharing our diverse experiences, so they are not lost. This memoir does not stand alone in the body of literary and dramatic texts that continue to rise from the ashes of those days. My hope is that it will contribute to our understanding of that time with a particular focus on the shared life of two people and the subsequent sole survivor who felt compelled to tell the story of their unusual journey.

Sharing these stories has revealed to me that they encourage each listener to reflect on their own experiences with loss, grief, and resilience. Alongside surprising moments of happiness and celebration, there is a distinct appreciation for life's absurdities. The mystery within these memories creates kinship among us, transforming despair and anger into hope and love.

1

Coughing. I woke up hearing him coughing.

Fever? Yes. A little one.

Chills? Yes.

Ok. It is winter. Flu season. He works in a medical lab. Sees tons of sick patients.

Nothing remarkable here.

"Raymond, stay home. You'll feel better after a day off. Do you want me to call in for you?"

I called in for him and he stayed home. I went to work. When I came home, he said he felt a bit better and we slept.

The next morning.

Hmmmmm. Not getting better.

It is January 1985. We don't for a moment consider the obvious. The obvious thought that is already running through your minds. The clarity of hindsight!

Like so many of us. We had had "the talk." This virus has a long incubation . . . even as long as two months! We had decided quite some time ago that we were *not* going to risk our lives in a world that had something this lethal in it.

Raymond was twenty-three when we met. I was twenty-two. He had had a "rich" experience as a young gay man in both San Juan, Puerto Rico, the island from which he came, and in New York City. He had run the gamut, and in many ways, he saw in me the opportunity to be with some – one. I, on the other hand, was newly awakening to my own nature and had embarked on a hearty exploration of what it all could mean.

I knew I loved him, but I wasn't ready to end my explorations just yet – to settle into exclusivity. But then, news of the virus came, and it seemed absurd not to heed the warning.

So, we pledged ourselves to each other. Happily. Knowing that by our decision we would *not* be affected by this thing. When two months passed, leaving us both well, and then more months and a few years passed, we honestly believed ourselves to be, as they say, in the clear.

Both of us are now in our late twenties. Fortunately, he had health insurance. I didn't. I worked for non-profits that weren't required to provide health insurance to employees. And what the hell – we were young and healthy. Neither of us had a regular doctor.

Three days. No improvement.

Off to the emergency room! X-Rays revealed nothing. Fever reduced. The cold walk to the bus in the midwinter weather had a positive effect. The doctor suggests, "This might be in your mind." We went home concerned, but no longer all that worried.

A few more days have passed. Symptoms are worsening.

Neither of us is satisfied with the diagnosis that these were imagined. And he was starting to have difficulty walking without breaking into coughing fits.

There was an old doctor, who still saw patients on the first floor of our apartment. Word around the building was that he was retired, a remnant of the glory days of the once elegant now dilapidating building.

I offered, "Let's go downstairs and see if he will see us."

He agreed, so down we went. The doctor was in.

For the first time, I experienced the "question" when we both sidled up to the receptionist seated at her desk. After getting his information, she looked at me over her reading glassed and asked, "And just who are you to him?" I repeated the words in my head – and just who are you to him. Not an easy question to answer at that moment. I stammered, "He's – my roommate. We live upstairs." Her response was a tossed off "Uh – Huh." And then she looked at me and said, "Well, you can sit out here and wait for him if you like."

He came out after about fifteen minutes, and we hurried back up to the apartment. He didn't say anything about the visit at first. When we got into our place I said, a bit impatiently, "So what did he say??"

"He wants me to go the hospital for tests."

I am a little alarmed, but say, "Good! Finally! We are going to get answers. This is good. You are gonna be fine. Let's get a bag packed for you."

In the bedroom, I pulled out a small carry-on bag. He was seated on the chair behind me. I'm packing his bag at the foot of the bed. My back is to him.

Silence.

Then – "James?" He called me James. To the world, I was Jim. But he said he wanted his own name for me and that he liked the name James and that was what he would call me. I loved him for it.

"James?"

"Uh-huh?" I turned to face him.

"He asked me if I am gay."

Punch in the gut . . . .

I sank down and sat on the edge of the bed. And in that moment – I knew.

He knew.

It was done.

But neither of us moved. Neither revealed the utter panic. The complete vulnerability. The death sentence. Life at that moment had transformed into a horror movie and we woke up finding ourselves in a cellar at 3:15 a.m. with all hell about to break loose.

"He asked me if I am gay."

"Raymond, this is a good thing," I lied. "He's a good doctor. He's making sure that every option is being considered. This is ok."

And I closed the bag.

He put on his winter jacket and his scarf. I put on mine. And together we left our apartment, locking the door behind us.

Who would we be the next time we came home together?

Who would we be – what would our lives have become?

We walked down the stairs, slowly, deliberately.

I got us a cab. No bus for this trip.

I opened the door to let him get in and closed it behind him. As I walked around the back of the cab and opened the door on my side – half in the cab and half out -the receptionist's question hovered in my mind.

"And just who are you to him?" she had asked.

Who are you to him?

And who is he to you?

2

"Probably infectious."

The old doctor had used the word – "infectious."

And for three days we waited. Waited for a clear diagnosis.

The "A" word was never uttered.

But there were other words – adjacent words – that kept bringing us closer to it.

Opportunistic.

Fungal.

Deficiency.

Viral.

Infectious.

And three days have passed.

The transition of life. We stood in the in-between. In between what life was and what life would become. A transitional moment. It was so hard to consider that we might, in fact, be saying goodbye to our old life. And we were frightened by this new one. This new life that was creeping in to take the old one's place.

I am alone in the apartment.

Looking around.

His aquarium. His hyacinth collection. Our music. Our two cats. All our stuff. My piano. Memories of the animals we sheltered here. Society finches. Gloucester canaries. The tarantula. The snakes. The cockatiels. The absurdity of everything that was. Only one thing was certain: everything needs disinfection. The application of chemicals will wipe away the invader that had entered our lives and set up residence in our home. Where was it lurking?

I prepped myself by putting on a mask, donning those stiff yellow kitchen sink gloves. I caught a look at myself in the big mirror and saw an alien in my own home.

The place was old. Cheap for the access it provided to Manhattan. Large for the $205.00 per month that would have been easily tripled just a few subways stops away on the other side of the Hudson River. Our hopes and dreams had been tied to the affordability of this place. And here I am attempting the impossible. I am attempting to clean a place that my grandmother would react to with a frown and say, "Jimmy. Some place just don't clean." Perfect. The impossibly infectious space that just won't clean. Yet this is my task. If this is an infectious disease, we must make sure it is no longer in the house! I had lived in these few rooms and had breathed the air of them constantly. If there was something to be afraid of in there, it had to have done its thing to me by now. But still, I am throwing things into hampers to go into the laundry, spraying cans of Lysol wildly, mixing bleach and water, dipping into the buckets with rags and sponges. "Be methodical!" I'm telling myself, "It's a chore . . . just do it." My mask in place, my gloves on, my chest pounding, and I am *not* crying. I am cleaning. Cleaning till I'm sweating. Cleaning. I am *not* crying. I am cleaning, trying to find hope in cleaning.

And the phone rings.

I pick it up.

The voice on the other end says, "Raymond has taken a turn for the worse. You need to get here right away."

I drop everything.

I rush out of the building and grab a cab to the hospital. Arriving there is surreal -moving through what seemed like a crowd congesting the ICU waiting area – like a subway car in rush hour. It is packed with people, but the noises they are making sound dull and impossible to understand. A nurse's hand grabs my arm and pulls me through the crowd of bellowing people. I hear her voice saying something like, "This is James! Let us through! He needs to see Raymond! Let him through!" Zombie-like, I follow her through the double doors of the entrance into the ICU.

There are no human sounds. But there are machine sounds, the unique sounds of medical monitors that track the journey of dwindling life. The beeps and buzzes and occasional alarms trigger white-coated activity. And in the corner of this sea of bays and beds is an odd glass bubble room. I can read the sign at its glass entry. "Isolation." The glass bubble of isolation contains a bed, and, on that bed, I can see Raymond's face – his eyes closed, lying on his back covered in a sheet up to his neck. And I am being led to the glass bubble room, and the door is opening and I am thrust inside. The door closes behind me, and he and I are left alone in the glass bubble room. The sound of the closing door jolts him and his eyes open.

He is calm.

I am projecting the same calm back to him.

"Hi."

"Hi."

I ask him, "How you doing?"

"Baby, I have AIDS."

Silence.

Adding hastily, "and you need to be checked out, too."

I brush off his concern, unwilling to become a target. Not yet. Please, not yet.

"I think I should go be with my parents in Puerto Rico. I think they will take me in."

I don't say anything.

He continues, "You need to get on with your life."

My brain rebels. He's telling me to get on with my life. What life is there without him?

Just. Who. Are. You. To. Me.

I don't fall in love easily, and God knows neither did he. But once I do, I am tenacious.

Finally, I spoke – with odd calm, "Y'know, if we were married, there would be no question about where you would stay. You would stay with me. In our home."

Silence.

And then I continued, "I'd like you to stay with me. If you want to. But if you want to go home, I won't stop you. But if you want to stay with me – well – I would like that. I would like that a great deal."

We had exchanged rings some years before, but what they would come to represent, we didn't fully realize. Probably like most young people looking for love, you think about finding a person you want to live with. But the question ultimately becomes, "Who will you die with? Who will you share *that* moment with?"

Raymond looked at me and he radiated relief. "I want to stay with you," he said.

And we touched and clinked our rings together in a gesture that years into the future I would repeat with my husband. "Wonder Twin Powers. Activate!"

And we smiled.

Inside a glass bubble room in the ICU of a Jersey City hospital, we received a terminal diagnosis—a moment that made February 14, 1985, a Valentine's Day I could never forget.

3

The next day.

Disoriented.

Unsteady.

Waking up blissful, without the memory of how life had changed. But in the early waking minutes that followed, the new reality came back with a thud.

I can't go to work. I do go to the hospital.

Once there, I get more news about what we are dealing with. This is PCP -Pneumocystis Carinii Pneumonia. A fungal infection, opportunistic, and treatable with some recent success. Raymond will have a 21-day course of injections with a drug called Pentamidine, which will, hopefully, rid him of this first AIDS-defining challenge and allow him to return home, until the next inevitable health crisis. While the doctor, still the old, wizened fellow from our apartment building spoke, I wondered why his eyes never met mine or why he never seemed to be talking to me or to Raymond, his patient.

As he was finishing his lecture on PCP and the chosen treatment, I realized that there were several nurses and interns listening – masked, gloved, robed. We all looked like refugees from a Twilight Zone episode. That's when a voice came into my ear. From behind. A woman's voice. She touched my arm with her gloved hand. Something told me to keep looking straight ahead and not back at her. And then her voice, in my ear, whispered, "You boys need a different doctor." I shuddered in confusion and she repeated slowly. "You boys need a different doctor." With that, the realization of what she was saying came to me and I turned to her and nodded my understanding, closing my eyelids slowly to suggest gratitude. She nodded back.

The group disbanded leaving me alone with Raymond.

What had just happened? For the first time of many times to come, the disease, itself, had "outed" us. We were no longer young men in a serious health crisis. We had been revealed as homosexuals with *that* disease. The illness was defining us. We were left there – humiliated: naked and unmasked. Raymond and I did not hide who we were or that we lived together and that we had a profound relationship. But we didn't have a name for it. I couldn't use the word boyfriend without feeling stupid. Lover felt melodramatic and absurd. Partner? – too corporate. Husband? Unthinkable at the time. All I knew was that he was "my person." And I was his. And that's all that mattered. He was far more aggressive in the world than I. If he experienced a whiff of judgement or hostility, his 5-foot 6-inch stocky body would whip around and begin a physical and verbal tirade that would intimidate and overwhelm the most offending homophobe. I was more content to keep the heat down in such moments and let them pass. Looking back, he was right – I was a bit of a wimp.

He was content to find himself in a community of homosexual people – gay people – he loved the discos, the music, the dancing, the whirl of celebration and playful hedonism that was the seventies. "C'mon James – let's go out! You will love it!"

"No, no. You go. Have a great time. I have stuff to do here."

Idiot! If only I could do that over!

Notions of *our* community. *our* tribe, *our* this or that meant nothing to me. I had found Raymond along the way and had fallen in love with him. And he with me. He knew my limits, I knew his extravagances, and we allowed both to exist. Because when we were in our apartment – our home – living our lives together, nothing else mattered. The rest was no one's business.

Or so I thought.

But now we had *our* virus and we needed reliable information. Facts. Ideas. Advice. We needed hope! There was no internet, no google search. We had newspapers, everything from the New York Times to the New York Native. And 800 numbers, most of which were populated with earnest people trying to make sure you were not successful at killing yourself. You might read, make calls, and receive both accurate information and misinformation. The word on the street conveyed doubtful wisdom, suggesting that phrases in the safe-sex guides like "multiple sex partners" did not refer to a series of one-on-one encounters but only to group experiences with several guys at once.

Distinguishing fact from fiction was next to impossible. Think about the intensity of Covid conspiracy theories – all of those dealing with a virus that had a 1 to 2 percent fatality rate. *Our* virus touted 100 percent fatality. Once you had it, you were as good as gone.

Here we are in a hospital with a well-meaning nurse whispering in my ear, "You boys need a different doctor." That simple sentence taught me everything. We were in peril. The judgement of others had power over us. We were unmasked and uncovered with an awareness that not everyone who should be on our side would be.

I believe that the virtue of courage can only exist in a person who understands and knows fear. Without fear, there can be no courage. In this moment, I was confronted with an overwhelming fear, but I didn't know if I could summon up enough courage to respond to it.

What I *did* know was that we were isolated, vulnerable, and alone. And I was scared. For us both.

4

The middle of the night.

And the voice on the 800 line gives me an address.

My half-awake brain hears a disembodied specter tell me to "Go there. You will find someone. Someone in your city. Someone who can help you."

The next morning is a Saturday.

I have no appointment.

I just went there. Early.

What was I looking for?

I knew I wanted competence. Someone who *knew* something. Someone who could tell me what to do. What to do *next.* I wanted a plan. Someone who could give me a plan to follow. A task list? A script! A "How To . . . " for God's sake.

I walked up the crumbly stone steps of the old town-house – now a "clinic." There is a makeshift sign out front that doesn't fill me with much hope. I try the door. It's open. I stepped into a dark foyer. A long staircase in front of me.

"Hello?"

So quiet. And then – a voice.

"Up here, honey. Just come right on up here."

The voice called down to me.

From that lilting soprano, I had an image of who he was.

And my spirits fell.

"No way. Really, no way could he be a person who could help me. He'd mean well. Sure. But *c'mon*!"

And then, suddenly, at the top of the stairs – there he was! The light behind him making his face hard to make out.

He saw me hesitate.

"Honey? Aw, honey. It's ok. You c'mon up now."

His southern affect was cute, but –

Ok. Be nice and just get on with it.

I made my way up the stairs of the old townhouse.

Each step. Each steep step.

"That's it," he said. "It's a long climb, but you gotta start somewhere," he drawled.

I continued my climb and took a moment to look up at him. I caught his eye and stopped dead in my tracks. He was staring at me. He met my eyes and I was looking directly into his.

And he had big eyes – full and knowing. And in that second, I melted.

I was fully aware that this staircase had become a ride – a ride that was going to be different from anything I had ever experienced before. This ride was going to change me. Change everything.

And it all started with climbing those stairs and following the sound of his voice.

And looking into his eyes.

I start to tremble.

He kept on talking, gently drawing me up to him. And my body starts freaking out. My legs are barely able to keep me upright and somehow – I make it up to the top of the stairs and his arms are open.

He is standing there. His arms open to me. Welcoming me into him. And I feel myself falling into his arms. And I am vibrating. My eyes are flooded, I can't see anything, and I am crying. Finally! Crying! And he is holding me, and we both fall from the weight of me onto the floor of the landing at the top of the stairs.

And he is rocking me.

"Oh, honey," he says, over and over and over.

And I cannot stop crying! But I am *there*! And he is there. And it is real. And in the moments that pass, I come to know what is ahead. It is a Saturday morning, I am in a townhouse clinic, and for this moment, he is my angel, one of many yet to come.

He lets me cry.

"Honey, you're crying for the life you had. Now you gotta get ready for the life that's coming in. Doesn't mean you won't cry some more – but you'll be laughing, too." And then he gives me telephone numbers. He makes me laugh and he says things. Some sassy things that make me laugh but I can't remember . . . .

And then he sends me out into the world.

I am not trembling.

Because of him, I am not trembling.

I am forever changed – by him.

"By you!" I think as I recall his face.

"Oh honey," I can hear you. Yeah.

Those eyes. I will remember his eyes forever.

Home was in his eyes.

Family, too.

I knew, for the first time that I belonged to a community of men who might make the choice to care for one another when the times demanded that care.

I was not alone. Raymond and I were not alone.

And I still remember his eyes.

His eyes meeting my eyes meeting your eyes.

Our eyes!

5

Five months have passed since diagnosis.

We have lived under a cloud of unknowing long enough to become uncomfortably accustomed to it. There were moments of absurd humor that underscored the direness of our plight and its relentless and stigmatizing impact.

Little jokes popped up in the community.

"What's that spot on your arm?"

"Oh that? It's either a pimple – or it's terminal cancer!"
BA-DUM-BUM

"What's the hardest thing about having AIDS?"

"Trying to convince your parents that you're Haitian!"
BA-DUM-BUM

Such was the nightmare of coming out to parents who often received news of their son's diagnosis coupled with the first realization that their son was a "homosexual."

The partner who fled? Yes, but there were many who did not abandon ship.

The parents who sent their kid packing? Yes, many. But there were many others who did not send their son into exile, but embraced him, stood by him, became his fiercest advocate, and made sure that every, albeit scant, medical option was available to him.

For every friend, who shrunk away in fear, there were more who stayed and cared for and watched and held hands with their comrade, who was now called part of the "walking wounded."

We militarized our role– those who were able-bodied, for the time being, had a front-line position, those who had passed demanded remembrance, and those who were sick were in the battle for their lives. But any one of them who managed to beat the thing could be the person who opened the door for everyone else to triumph. Every person who was sick was, therefore, a symbol of hope – if only – if only they might survive. In 1985, few with full blown AIDS did. The path was clear. We were in the fight of our lives and against all the odds, we summoned up an arrogant will to believe we could beat those impossible odds. Or die trying.

Five months in and I became strategic!

I had been in a GMHC – Larry Kramer's Gay Men's Health Crisis – support group that met once a week. Good, kind, smart, New York City men taking care of their partners – doing the right thing for lovers, ex's, boyfriends, or men who loved each other but defied being labeled. We met every week under the watchful eye of a social worker. He encouraged us to use our person's frequent time away during the inevitable hospitalizations as an opportunity to rehearse their inevitable death.

I found the whole idea deplorable!

The room felt beaten down, resigned. A room full of smart, resourceful, resilient gay men now seemed scared, despairing, and defeated.

One guy spoke about his lover's recent death. It had happened while he was away from the hospital and by the time he got back, the body was gone. He never got to see his lover's dead body – just the clean sheets of the newly-made bed that had supported his lover's final moments. He never got to see the body. He became obsessed and we all knew that he would be haunted by that empty bed for as long as he lived. I think every one of us swore to ourselves that that would not happen to us.

In the weeks that passed, it became clear to me that New York City was becoming overrun. Everywhere in the city you can feel a growing desperation. The idea of escape became increasingly real. We had a support system in Washington D.C. I had done my undergraduate years there – had worked for the Smithsonian for a year before moving to the New York City area, returning to D.C. for two years of grad school before returning home to Jersey City. Five months into this journey, it felt like our Jersey City apartment was going to be our tomb and that we would be trapped in it because there was nowhere else to go except for a hospital emergency room, where we would make repeated visits until whatever was ailing him could not be treated and the journey would end. And mine might begin?

We were told that the process could take about eighteen months. Five had already passed. Lucky thirteen to go.

I said to him, "Raymond, let's get the fuck out of here."

"Where will we go?"

"Let's go down to D.C. I can get us an apartment. I have a ton of friends there. You already know a lot of them. There aren't as many cases. NIH is there. We might have a fighting chance. Here, it's bad. The town is overwhelmed. It can't handle it. If we stay here –" I broke off.

He thought for a few minutes and finally turned up to me and said, "Let's do it."

The next morning, I called friends there, who were vacating their apartment. We figured out how we could move in right away. My primary work was portable, and its home base was in D.C. anyway. My life in New York City was an accommodation by the company that allowed me to live in the city which held the opportunities for my professional and artistic dreams to come true. But I knew they would welcome me back with the force of a homecoming. I knew we would be safer there. And in the five months since his diagnosis, most of the people down there knew what was going on with us, so we would be spared the endless and exhausting process of "coming out" with AIDS to a whole new set of people.

I got a U-Haul. It all felt exhilarating. We were gonna make a break! Make an escape! Who knows? We might even leave the illness behind, too! By changing our circumstances, might we beat the odds?

It felt like magic.

Our friends in New York City didn't know. And I called our closest and told her, "We're heading to DC. We're going to see how things go down there. We may come back – we may not." And she said, "Are you moving there? And I stammered "I don't know, but we are *going* there." And she said, "Do you have a truck?" and I said, "Yes." And the final question, "Are you taking the piano with you?" and I said, "Yes, it's in the truck." And she said, "You're moving." And I said, "I guess we are."

Years later, a friend of mine asked me, "Why was it so difficult to admit that you were moving? Was there shame in it?" I had to think about it for a long time because the moment was loaded and the reasons were many.

The move acknowledged that we were afraid. We were running, like refugees, hoping for rescue in exile. Perhaps, more importantly, leaving New York City was giving up on a dream, to accept that the future you had in mind, the future you were working towards, simply wasn't going to happen. Imagine being a farmer, who after years of effort had established a fertile acre of ground that was finally yielding, showing the rewards of all the time and effort. At harvest time, an unexpected fire erupts and burns it all away. And you know you have to move on. But the effort, the care, the hopes buried in that scorched earth are hard to walk away from.

Like so much of that period – nothing seemed completely real. You went through the motions of life, but you were living in a strange in-between place. Caught there, still breathing – in a world occupied by normal, healthy people, who were not all that concerned about the impact of this new virus. They would be safe if they kept their distance from people like us. But there were many who opened their arms and hearts and held us through the journey.

We drove down the New Jersey Turnpike, and over the Delaware Memorial Bridge, and down Route 95, through the Baltimore Tunnels, inside the Capital Beltway, right up to the District line and landed in the parking lot of the garden apartment that would be our new home.

On the drive down, we laughed – with a robustness that I hadn't experienced in five months. We sang along with the radio, and we bantered and attempted to provoke each other with digs about our personalities – all the normal stuff that one does on a road trip.

It felt like we were coming alive again.

Might we have left that virus and its death sentence behind? Had we escaped? Was this some kind of miracle, or strange mind-over-matter success?

The answer? Yes. And no.

Something about that move stimulated a period of relative health and peace. It was a hopeful time that lasted for about a year. A good year without hospitalizations. Good doctors. We met Larry, our wonderful, young, gay, "take on the world" doctor, who was as invested in "beating the thing" as we were. He was smart and savvy and cocky and could tell the difference, intuitively, between what experimental treatment showed promise with acceptable risk and those that revealed *some* promise with **un**acceptable risk.

We were lab rats. So the guy running the experiments had to be trustworthy.

And we believed he was.

And for the next five years, we built a caring partnership that saw Raymond through many trips to the emergency room, many hospitalizations, many trials – the first AZT trial when the drug was then called Compound S, which I would pick up in a white paper bag from the pharmacy at the Washington Hospital Center. So clandestine!

The result? Anemias, transfusions, spinal taps, cultures, fevers, IV antibiotics, and prophylactic oral meds to stave off the PCP that almost did him in at the beginning. Through it all, though, we felt like a fight was on. Every day we survived, we knew we weren't winning, but we were still in the game. A thirteen-month prognosis extended to twenty-four. And two years became three years – and while it was a struggle – the clock was able to amaze us as it tracked the daily success story of his survival. And three years became four years – and another Christmas – and another New Year.

6

1986. To test or not to test? Is it better to confront the fact that mortality now walks undeniably beside you each day? Or is it better to live without that certain knowledge?

Raymond had the test, once-and-for-all to confirm what we already knew. Yes, the positive result confirmed our reality. There had been no mistake, there would be no stunning miracle of science that could tell us that it had been a mistake, a misdiagnosis. No. The test confirmed what we already knew.

But what about *me*? Why was I resisting getting that test? Why wouldn't I want to know my status? For certain. That was the word – to this day – status – what is your status? Something troubling about it. Status.

The answer for me was not complicated. Not knowing left me with the possibility that I might *not* be infected.

In my mind, taking the test would more than likely demolish that hope. How could I *not* be positive? Absurd. But, not knowing for sure left the door open to that possibility. And through it: a kind of weird hope. Only the test could reveal the truth – that hope was futile.

Plus, what could you do with a positive result? *Nothing*! What did they say? "Avoid stress and its adverse effects on the immune system." Avoid stress? Hmm. Which is more stressful: to confront the certainty of impending doom, or to endure the anxiety of uncertainty and cling to improbable hope?

I knew myself well enough to know that having the news-certain would send me into a tailspin. It would hasten my demise. And the shift to concerns about my own health would not be good for Raymond. I had to stay well. I had to maintain the illusion of health to myself and to the world. That illusion might become a delusion of health, but nevertheless a necessary one. He needed me healthy to keep us on track. I did not resist. I would hope that I was not infected, but I would live as though I *were* infected. I would live as though *everyone* was infected. They had a name for that, too. Universal Precaution. I was all for that! My rationale for escaping the moment of truth was complete.

I did come to realize that the illusion of health is all any of us ever has. It lets us sleep at night, lets us dream, lets us live inside the realm of life's possibilities without the certainties of assured mortality that come when the illusion is shattered.

Dr. Larry asked me to consider getting tested. I knew that as our doctor, he really wanted to know where I stood. But I wouldn't give permission. He suggested a compromise and said, "Can I at least test your T-cell levels?" Illogically, I said, "Yes, you can do that." I knew if the T-cells were low, there was an issue, but if the T-cells were high, it would support my fantasy of escape. Confoundedly, without any guarantee of anything.

On Christmas Eve, he called and left a message on my answering machine. "Jim. It's Larry. I wanted to let you know that your T-cell test came back and your numbers are just fine – more than fine, they are excellent. Merry Christmas!" What a relief! It was not a release from the possibility (in my mind the certainty) of infection, but it did give me the one thing valued most by all of us in our circumstance – *time.* I would have more time. Time enough to see Raymond through this? I hoped. But what would come after? I simply refused to think about it. Just don't think about it.

You have time. Use it well.

This was 1986. By 1987 there was a change.

Compound S!

Later called AZT, ironically a drug resurrected as an old and ineffective cancer treatment from twenty years earlier. AZT proved itself to be effective at fighting HIV. It was the first drug to prove "efficacy" (another word that became frequently used in the AIDS era's evolving vocabulary). You might be able to extend your life expectancy by six to eight months with full-blown AIDS, and you might be able to delay the progression of HIV disease into the defining fatal syndrome for a longer time.

My excuse was gone.

I went to see Larry and told him I had changed my mind. With the news of AZT, I had no logical way to avoid the test. I would know I was positive, but I would have the benefit of taking a drug that might help me live long enough to see the next drug and the drug after that and after that. There was a clock to beat after all!

Jason, the staff nurse in Larry's office, took my blood and displayed his usual light and airy approach to life in the belly of the beast. He gave me a look and said, "The hard part is waiting two weeks for the result to come back. Sorry about that."

Two Weeks. I will not forget how slow those days passed waiting for the inevitable news. Raymond knew I had been tested and knew how long it would take to learn the results. We didn't talk about it much. We just let the hours go by, the days go by. Inevitably, the word would come.

I went to work every day. We didn't have the luxury of not working. The rent had to be paid. The utilities. There were bills. And there was a value in working while in a crisis. It gave you something to focus on other than yourself, or the illness, or the tedious hopelessness that you tried to beat away each day. I worked for a theater company, an endeavor that was no stranger to the impact of this plague. We were fortunate enough to have a place of employment that provided empathy and flexibility that was an enormous support for us both. Raymond was welcome to come and do volunteer work. He became a character around the office. People grew to love him. He knew how to engender that in people. He knew his survival depended on it.

At last, the two weeks were up. The day had arrived. I left the office at lunch time, saying I was going out to run an errand. No one at work knew about my test or my purgatory of waiting. I got in my car and started driving. Where was I going? Nowhere in particular. I had to call into the doctor's office to get the results. No cell phones back then. I didn't want to call from work. And I didn't want to call from home. And the doctor's office was too far away to go there to get the news in person. So, I pulled into the parking lot of the Wheaton, Maryland International House of Pancakes, parked the car and got out a quarter to put into the payphone in the booth just outside the entrance.

Pat, the receptionist, answered the phone – always nice. "Oh – hi Jim. I'll put you through to Jason." "Thanks, Pat." I said casually and warmly. Then the silence of the hold button. The longest forty-five seconds of my life. Then the click. "Jim?" It was Jason. "Hi, Jason." Without skipping a beat, he said. "I have your results. Do you want them over the phone?"

Alarm! Alarm! If they say that it is probably bad news!

I laughed a little and choked out, "Oh, what the hell, Jason, just tell me what's up."

He paused for about five seconds, and I could hear the rustling of papers. Then he said, "There you are." And another five seconds of silence. He was reading. "Jim? You're still negative."

That was it. My life changed forever, yet again.

"Jim. You're still negative."

For some reason, I didn't want to overreact. "Oh, that's good news, Jason. Thank you." My hand trembling. And then – "Jason? *Still* negative? What do you mean?" "Your first test last year was negative, and your current test is still negative." And then it hit me. Larry had my blood tested for HIV when he said he was checking my T-cell counts. He absolutely went ahead with it without my permission. If it had come back positive, I bet he would have convinced me to get tested.

I couldn't be mad at him. In fact, I loved him for it. He left himself open to a lawsuit because he cared so much. I love him for it. I have had many teachers who taught me the science of art – a method of approaching it with intelligence, context, process. But Larry was a man of science, of medicine, who had the extraordinary ability to teach me the art of science: the practice of medicine with deeply human instincts, intuition, sensitivity, even improvisation. Being in his care was a gift to treasure.

I didn't go back to work. I decided to go home. There was cause to celebrate! The unthinkable had happened. I was frigging *negative*! How could it be? I felt something lift off me that left me light and young and silly and giddy. I was elated. And I wanted to get home and share – my reverie suddenly starting to change on my five-mile ride home.

I arrived. Raymond was sitting on the couch in the living room, watching TV. He knew today was the day. And he was anxious. He wanted good news. And he didn't think we were going to get it, either. I turned off the TV and stood there and said simply – "I got the result. It's negative. I'm negative." His eyes closed in relief and his body relaxed into peace. And I was relieved. On one level, we were both released from the other horrible thought that either of us could have given the thing to the other. My result took that unspoken possibility off the table. However this thing came into our lives, I had not given it to him, and he had not given it to me (ruefully wondering why that even mattered given our ignorance of its existence.)

But when his eyes opened – with every attempt to hide it from me – and every attempt on my part to not see it – his eyes revealed an utter loneliness. The recognition that, while we were in this together, it was somehow different. He was positive and I was negative. He did not luck out. I did luck out. And the illness tried again to do the thing it was so good at doing – keeping us from each other, keeping us removed from each other, keeping us from loving each other.

I sat down next to him on the couch and said, "I'm so happy that we don't have to worry about me. I can work. I can keep us going. And you can focus on getting well. You are going to beat this. And I am in it with you. We're better off as a team with this result. It's better for both of us. And he acknowledged that what I was saying was true. But, dammit, I had seen the realization in his eyes that surprised even him when the news of how we were different made him – angry, not sad, but in a weird and inescapable way – alone.

7

1989. And the numbers of the diagnosed continue to grow exponentially and the number of deaths is horrific. And yet, we survive another day.

Along the way, you become strongly attached to friends engaged in the same fight. You became brothers with them as you compare your journey, talk about side effects, opportunistic infections, weight loss, pain, do you have Kaposi's Sarcoma, the lethal cancer that was also AIDS-defining. Or are you spared, like Raymond, the tell-tale red splotches that are the vivid hallmark of the disease's progression?

Michael was one of our comrades. A promising actor, a bit younger than us by about two years. He was diagnosed a year or so after Raymond. Michael was a pistol. Sharp-tongued, dry-witted, smart, clever, a delight to be with, Michael and Raymond loved to keep abreast of each other. Like two racehorses that cooperate at keeping pace with each other, caring more about winning the race together than beating each other out in competition. It seemed like the two would continue to be in that race together for some time and I know that Raymond found an enormous strength in the fact that his friend Michael was doing well. If two could beat it that would be better than just one. This virus is not as invincible as it appears to be.

Springtime came and it was Easter Sunday. Michael's health had deteriorated during that last year. And on Easter Sunday, he was living at his family home. Friends came to visit and he was lying outside on a beautiful and warm spring day. He told them that he had gotten up that morning and put on his lucky red socks. "Because when you have your lucky red socks on, nothing really bad can happen to you." And, it was Easter, after all!

Michael died that afternoon.

I got a call – *the* call as we would say – from Barbara, who had been with him earlier that day. She said that it had been peaceful. And when I got off the phone, I hated the task of telling Raymond. I shared the news, which at this point was not a big surprise.

But death, no matter how inevitable, always comes as a surprise. With it comes the end of hope for more tangible life. While the person continues to breathe, there is still hope—no matter how unfounded—that somehow the dying person might inexplicably rally. Sometimes, in a quiet room, you can hear each shallow breath and find yourself holding your own, listening for any change. In those moments, even the faintest stir—a flutter of eyelids or the grip of a hand—feels like a promise that they might be okay, if only for a little while longer.

But no, no – that was not going to be. Raymond had lost a brother-in-arms.

And later that night, when we were trying to fall asleep, I could sense that he was awake and restless. I got up and sat on the edge of his side of the bed and asked him how he was doing and if Michael's passing was keeping him awake. He said he was going to miss Michael and that he felt that with Michael gone, he was next on the list to go – and that he really didn't want that and that he didn't want his life to be over.

I grasped at straws saying something about how every health journey is different, that just because a bad thing happens to one person, it doesn't mean that it will happen to you. Blah, blah, blah. But he heard me and breathed it in, because, frankly, there was nothing else to breathe in.

He said that he would miss talking to Michael.

Raymond slept next to a big double window that looked out to a fire escape. And in the April night, we both got up to look out that window and take in the cloudless night sky, filled with stars. Orion the Hunter hung above the horizon like he does, in full view. And I said to Raymond, "Look! There's our old friend Orion." And he said, "Yes, I see his belt." Then suggestively, "I always see his belt." I laughed. And then I asked him if he wanted to pick one of those stars in Orion's belt as a spot that he could talk to Michael. He nodded and said, "I'm going to go for that middle star." And I said, "No surprise there!"

And we laughed again.

But, soon after, we got quiet and we decided to call it Michael's Star. And from that night on, Raymond had his companion and friend Michael, up in the night sky, forever available to him – that middle star in the belt of Orion.

8

May 1990. Unbelievable. He has survived more than five years.

Research is moving. If you can just stay alive – just a few more years – you might make it. This was unthinkable one year ago. Progress is slow, but the ideas are in place. Effective treatment, not a cure – yet – but a viable strategy for turning this viral death machine into something chronic and manageable. That was the phrase. With effective treatment, AIDS might become a chronic manageable disease.

Those three words put together sounded beautiful. Uplifting! Not far out of reach. They gave us a reason to stick around. A reason to continue to fight. A reason to dare to hope.

Some days would pass and the terror of it all was starting to morph into something new. Still challenging, still scary, but there was a light on the horizon. The kind of light you perceive while it is still night, but you know that there is a sun down there, under the horizon line, and it is going to rise.

I was at my desk at the office when the phone rang.

"Hello, Jim here."

"Hi."

"Oh, hi! You OK?"

"Yes. But something happened."

"OK. Calm down. Are you OK?"

"Yes."

"OK. Tell me."

"I wanted to call you. But I couldn't remember who you were. And then – I couldn't remember who I was. I couldn't remember anything about anything."

"Do you now?"

"Yes."

"You know I am on speed dial. All you have to do is push 'one' and my phone here will ring. Make a little sign and put it next to the phone- To reach James – press 1."

"OK."

"I'm going to call Larry. Stay put. I will be home as soon as I can."

"OK."

I called Larry. Pat put me right through to him.

"Hi Larry. I just got off the phone with Raymond. He sounded worried. He said that for some time this morning, he couldn't remember who he was. I thought I should call you."

I waited to hear the theory of the latest opportunistic infection and what we might need to do to combat it. I would get prepared. Get Raymond prepared. Begin the next search for information. Fight this next challenge.

But there was a long pause.

And finally, the sound of a sigh on the phone. Uncharacteristic. And then Larry said to me, so gently,

"Jim . . . Raymond needs you for just a little while longer."

And everything stopped.

"Oh. Oh...Yes. Do you want me to bring him in?

"Sure."

"OK. Thanks. Bye."

I hung up the phone.

Raymond needs me for just a little while longer.

I put my head down on my desk.

The following day, I took him to see Larry. He looked him over and said to us that he suspected a condition called PML.

Progressive.

Multi-focal.

Leukoencephalopathy.

A viral disease of the brain. Basically, from what I could understand, it was an evolving illness that left lesions that turned the brain into a kind of Swiss cheese, leaving a variety of symptoms. There was no known treatment. Life expectancy? Three months. In short, I learned that PML was the infection that killed the patients who managed to survive everything else that this syndrome could throw at them. This was going to be the end of the line.

In the weeks that followed, Raymond developed signs of dementia, an inability to use his left side, and a halting and labored speech pattern. He spoke in such a deliberate way. If he over-articulated every word he said, then he could make himself understood.

And he really wanted to be understood.

Larry advised me to get prepared for the inevitable.

I heard him, but I can't get there. I had developed a habit of responding to each challenge.

Do the research.

Find a patient who had survived for longer than expected.

Learn about what they did.

Present the material to Larry.

See what we can do.

I found the patient. Alive with PML for two years! He was taking a drug called cytosine arabinoside. Some other drugs, too. There was a lead! Even though it didn't work on anyone else, it did work in this one case. Could we pursue it? Larry was skeptical, but willing to try.

It was now early August. Raymond developed a fever and concern for other infections led him to be hospitalized. He was there for five days. I went into hospital mode. Go in the late afternoon, two hours before dinner and spend that time with him. On this day, I walked into his room. It was rather grand. Because of the practice of isolating AIDS patients, he was often relegated to the fancier sections of the hospital, where well-heeled patients who could afford single rooms would stay. He was just one of several patients with AIDS who found themselves in what seemed like a room in a grand hotel. The opulence felt strangely out of place, a stark contrast to the isolation and uncertainty that hung in the air.

When I walked into his room, he was busy. Chatting away, saying things I couldn't understand. When he caught my eye, he stopped suddenly and said,

"Hi, James."

"Who are you talking to?"

"My friends," he offered reluctantly.

"And who might they be?"

"There's Helen the Hawaiian. There's the Mauri warrior."

And there was a third visitor that I cannot remember who Raymond said they were.

"We are making a lei out of frangipani blossoms." He was gushing. "They are very beautiful."

"Are your friends still here?"

"They are hiding."

"Oh!"

He whispered their conspiracy, "They are hiding in the bathroom," pointing to the closed door of the bathroom across from the bed. "No one is supposed to know they are here. It's amazing, James! When they are here, I can speak and move and think. Everything works!"

"Well, that's great. When I leave you can go back to making your garland with them."

The next day, I returned to a more sullen version of himself.

"How are you doing?"

"OK."

"Where are your friends?"

"They aren't coming back."

"Why not?"

"Because I told. I wasn't supposed to tell. So, they aren't coming back. They said they can't."

"Listen – what if we decide to never speak of them again? Do you think they might come back then?" I said it, hoping that the idea would be greeted as a promising strategy. But, instead, he looked right into my eyes and said, sadly and simply, "Oh no, James. You don't get a second chance."

Two days later, August 8 – He was released to come home. This was the first time he left the hospital in wheelchair, a practice he never allowed. But now, he had no choice. I pushed the chair while he sat with a plant in his lap. It was a gift from a friend. He was taking it home. But suddenly, he asked me to stop when he saw a young man walking toward us in the corridor by the elevators. He handed the plant to the young man and said firmly, "Give it to the lady with AIDS in the room next to mine." I looked into the room and saw an emaciated 18-year-old girl looking pale and hollow lying on the bed. The young man assured Raymond that the plant would be delivered.

Raymond seemed satisfied and said, "Thank you for staying awake with me all night! James, this is Pablo – he stayed awake with me all night!" he said with enthusiasm.

"Thank you, Pablo," I said resolutely.

And then, Raymond summoned up all his dignity. Gripping the arm rests to help him sit as upright in his wheelchair as he could and spoke, "I will remember you for the rest of my life."

It was an extraordinary moment. This dying man, with a life-expectancy of about five minutes, promised to remember his caring nurse for the rest of his life. And it seemed important and monumental! Pablo smiled and touched Raymond's hand as we rolled out of his life and into the elevator and into the world for one last time.

The next week, now relegated to his bed in our bedroom, he became increasingly aware that the time was short. He asked me to dial up his family in Puerto Rico. I did and handed him the cordless phone with the antenna fully extended. He was agitated.

"When are you coming?" He spoke with heat. "When are you coming?" His face darkened as he heard an answer he didn't like. "You have to come soon. If you don't come soon, there will be no reason to come at all!"

He was yelling at the phone and then suddenly threw it across the room where it smashed against the plaster wall and broke into useless plastic pieces.

The energy of the phone smashing against the wall calmed him and he was lying on the bed. Spent, I sat down on the floor, my back against the side of his bed.

Just breathing.

Out of the corner of my eye, I saw his hand floating off the mattress. Suspended in space. Limp but present. And I wanted to feel his hand. And I reached over and lifted his hand and put it on the top of my head. And he let it stay there. And I could feel him moving his hand across the top of my head. Less than an inch of movement. He was petting my head. And then I hear him call as if into a long unfathomable distance.

"James?"

"Yes, honey. I'm here."

"James??"

"Yes, I'm here."

"James???"

"I'm here."

9

We stopped sleeping in the same bed. His dementia left him flailing wildly during the night. And "accidents" became so common that they couldn't be called accidents anymore. But we shared our room. Twin beds, like dormitory roommates. More like *Ozzie and Harriet*, our bedroom resembled a bizarre sit-com set that ensured appropriate separation. It was half *Father Knows Best* and half *General Hospital.* But I could see him across the small room. We always had a night light on. I needed that. I had re-found my childhood fear of the dark and silence. I would sometimes be surprised, waking up to see him staring at me. It was not a stare of recognition or observation. It was the look that someone has when they are trying to figure out what they are seeing. I'm not even sure he was seeing anything that was real – tangible – in the room. Me. But he was trying to make out something, *understand* something. Words became utterances. Gestures became spasms.

And breathing seemed no longer involuntary, but rather an act of will.

We lived this way for a few weeks. And then, one night, I woke up to a strange, gurgling sound – a sound I had never heard before. Glancing at the digital clock – 3 a.m. The night light revealed a strange silhouette. What I thought I was seeing didn't make sense, but the noise I was hearing sounded like an alarm. Suddenly, I am wide awake and reaching for the lamp. A blast of light – and there he was – flopped face up. His back arched – his arms outstretched and taut – his legs quivering – intensely. Eyes open. Staring up at the ceiling. Head bent back – mouth wide open.

Out of his mouth spewed a red geyser that shot – forcefully – more than three feet into the air. The only sound was the endless choking, gurgling drone that was connected to "The Blood Fountain."

Looking at it, I am frozen. A simple moment of stunned paralyzing fright. In 1990, hatefully, a blood fountain pouring out of the mouth of a person with AIDS made any intimate moment of physical comfort something you had to consider carefully. Consider the risk.

FUCK!

What do I do with this? I looked up to the same ceiling he was looking at, shouting, "What do you want me to do with this?" Don't ask me who I was talking to.

I don't believe in it.

But I do believe in it.

But I don't.

I picked up the new nearby cordless. Larry's home number was now on speed dial.

"Larry – it's Jim. It's awful. The blood – it's shooting up out of his mouth. I don't know what to do. I don't know what to do!"

"Jim. Calm down. Calm down. Breathe."

Just the sound of his voice had a good effect on me.

"Jim. This is nearing the end."

"I know. I know! What do I do?"

"Have you called for an ambulance?"

"No! No! He wants to go from home. He wants to die at home! He told me! He doesn't want to go to the hospital!"

A short silence . . . and then –

"Jim. I am going to take this out of your hands. I am going to call for an ambulance. He will have an easier time at the hospital. Let's try to make this as easy as possible for *him*."

"Yes. Yes. Please. Yes – thank you!"

I was losing the war.

I was wandering through the debris of a bombed-out field – flailing at an enemy that was already celebrating its victory. I am defeated. Then, something new. I heard – silence. No more choking sounds. Was it over? Was it over while I was talking to Larry on the phone? Was he gone? I looked at him. Still breathing. But the rigidness of his body was gone. He was almost peaceful. The blood fountain had passed and was replaced by something calm – his body – limp – collapsed.

I sat on the bed and waited for the ambulance, throwing on clothes. In the heat of a D.C. late night in August – that was a pair of shorts, a T-shirt, and a pair of flip-flops. How I loved those hot nights! And I grew as calm as he was, sitting on the edge of my bed, looking across at him. And I'm thinking, "Raymond – these are probably our last minutes in our bedroom." And all our bedrooms came into my head. The one in Newark when we first met, our Jersey City apartment, our first place when we moved to D.C. after he was diagnosed, and now the one in the little house we bought to weather the storm. All were different and yet all the same. Because they were *our* room.

I wanted to thank all the rooms that had sheltered us! And tonight, we will leave our room for the last time.

The ambulance arrived and the guys came in. I was ready for anything. We still couldn't count on an even remotely civil encounter with people whose job it was to take care of us. No. You could not count on that. But these guys seemed different. They were kind. They seemed to know the stakes of what was happening.

They put him on a gurney, shooing away our three puppies who kept wanting to play. They would jump on Raymond trying to hold him in place. But not tonight. I hurriedly caged the dogs while the guys got Raymond into the ambulance. Larry had asked them not to put on any flashing lights or sirens. They had complied. I asked if I could travel with them, but they said that wasn't possible. I didn't ask why. I simply said, "I'll follow in my car." I was compliant. I went back into the house, released the dogs who ran upstairs to their preferred spots on the beds. I shut the door behind me and climbed into my red Hyundai Excel – the first of many that I would buy throughout my life. I am a loyal idiot. And I followed the ambulance that was carrying the dearest part of my life to his deathbed. Driving away from our little house, I looked at it in the darkness and remembered how we laughed at its whimsy. It was an extremely modest, urban, architectural folly. We described it as "the little Cape Cod with Tudor affectations." We were leaving it, driving away for the last time.

I needed something to happen! Something rich – fantastical. I knew it was too much to ask, but I needed it. I looked upward yet again. "Give me something, dammit! Something! *I am lost!*"

And in return, there was only the sound of a weak Hyundai motor hurtling us forward on the ten-minute drive to the Washington Hospital Center.

To fill the silence, I clicked on the radio. It was already tuned to my classical music station. I heard music.

"No!"

In disbelief, I laugh as I hear the climactic strains of the Tchaikovsky Violin Concerto – one of Raymond's most favorite pieces of music. And there it was – at its climax. And it was beautiful and profound and big. It is *huge music*! And there it was on the radio in my red Hyundai, during a steaming hot August night on the road to God knows what.

I do believe in it.

But I don't believe in it.

But I do.

The ambulance speeds ahead and goes into the bowels of the building where I cannot take my car. I am happy he is here. They will help him through this. It is the right decision. I hope it is the right decision. I'm thinking, "What if he wakes up? Suddenly fully lucid? Looking at me!

"James! What the fuck am I doing in this miserable hospital? I told you . . . "

I laughed at the thought of his reprimand. And said to the specter, "I am doing the best I can! You – You are throwing stuff at me and I can't keep up!" But in my head, we are both smiling – teasing – pretending an annoyance that wasn't really there – like we had done for years – like we do.

And I snap to. Parking the car in the satellite parking lot and walking toward the brightly lit Emergency sign just ahead.

I went in and walked up to the front desk. At this hour, the place, normally bustling, was oddly quiet. How many times have we been here? How many times did I sit with him for hours as the slow progress of emergency room care took its own sweet time?

The young man at the desk looks up at me. "Can I help you?"

"Yes. I'm here to be with Raymond Davila. He was just brought in by ambulance."

He looked down and then back at me. "He's here alright. Your relationship to the patient?"

Always a trick question.

"I'm his partner. His significant other. His . . . " I'm stammering. I know this is not going well.

The dude smears a half sneer onto his face and says, "Sorry, you need to be a relative to go in there." His look revealed that he was enjoying the pain he was inflicting on me. Perhaps even feeling a bit virtuous by his stringent following of the rules. But mostly, he enjoyed exerting his power over me. One of the fags.

I offer, "I've been in this emergency room many times without a problem." Sweet as pie.

"Well, not tonight." This was his final answer as he looked down and away from me.

I wanted to fly into a rage. Scream at this fool. Rail against his unjust power over me – over us. But I just stood there frozen.

"Jim," I said to myself, "don't let this moment be about this guy. Just go with it."

And I calmed myself and started breathing more normally.

But I said one last thing to him. "When does your shift end?"

He looked up and said "6 a.m." And I said, "Thank you," and walked to the waiting area, where a television set, high up in the air, was blaring some unwatchable bullshit. I sat down. Calmly. My eyes are half-closed. And I'm thinking about Raymond. I'm sending my thoughts to him – down the hall – through the walls – to whatever bed he was lying in – unconscious – waiting to die. And I'm thinking, "Honey, I am here. I am right here. I am right next to you." In some unexplainable way, the words were true. But I am counting the minutes until 6 a.m.

Out of the blue, the thought hits me. "So, this is marriage!" *This* is what marriage is at its most fully realized. We are inseparable. The clucking world can do nothing to us. And with that realization, I was suddenly – oddly – really – OK.

10

6 a.m. came. The sunlight brought with it a new energy. What would this day bring? Death is more at one with night. With the light of day, there seems to be greater possibility for more life. Or is that wishful thinking?

The young woman who had replaced my nemesis from a few hours ago, was kind. I explained to her who I was and how her predecessor on the night shift had decided to block my entry to Raymond's room. She was horrified. And she said, "I'll get you in there quickly." I said, "Thank you." But then I stopped her and spewed, "You know, I want to thank you for your kindness, but my life and Raymond's life should not be dependent on the kindness that the person at this desk has or chooses to have in these moments. You're terrific and I am grateful for you, but this should not be about how kind a person you are, or anyone is! What happened here tonight was just plain wrong!"

I was speaking angrily to a person who had been kind, but I had spared the person who did the evil deed itself. Hmmm. She did not flinch but instead nodded in understanding and went off to get me access to the room.

She was back in less than a minute and said, "He's right in here." I moved toward his bay, turned the corner, and found him lying there. Peaceful. Breathing easily with an oxygen tube in his nose. Nothing else. A nurse walked in and I stammered, "What's that hose for? I don't want this prolonged!" I was snappish, but she was easy and said, "This won't make it take any longer, but it will make it easier." And I softened and said, "Oh. Yes. Easier. I want that. I want it to be easier. As easy as possible. Thank you. I'm sorry." I looked back at him and put my hand on top of his and sighed.

"I'm here."

We stayed in the emergency bay for a few hours, but he stabilized and we were moved to a regular room. He wasn't hooked up to anything. No fluids, no antibiotics, no pain medication that I could identify. A reclining chair was brought into the room for me. I was told I could spend the night here. It became clear that this had become a vigil. I was here to wait and to watch. As the day wore on, the occasional friend would stop in for a few minutes. Barbara arrived, hell-bent to see it through to the end with us. I don't recall our conversations. I felt separated from the world of the living. The people who had lives, who did things, had jobs, had tasks. I had no task but to sit and watch and wait and I wanted the whole world to sit and stop and wait with me. Because he deserved the attention.

I had had five years to prepare for this day. Why did it seem so remote? So unexpected? So unrehearsed?" How far removed was I from the person who had been concerned about Raymond's wishes to die at home? Larry had been right. Raymond was exactly where he needed to be. And so was I.

Inevitably, his vitals weakened as we moved into another night. I don't recall eating anything that day or sleeping since early in the night before. I was utterly exhausted. I felt a part of me leaving the world. I had one foot in this world and the other in the next. Some part of me was with him – moving forward into an unknown. And I drifted into sleep, lying on the recliner, next to his bed – both of us unconscious, spent, powerless. Submitting to whatever was going to happen next.

But Barbara remained alert. The angel present. Awake, alert, ministering over the crumpled and impotent bodies of her two friends. She stood watch over us. Later, she told me about one moment where he seemed to awaken and she told him, "James is right here. Next to you. He's right here." She said she saw a single tear fall from his right eye and down his cheek and then he went back to sleep.

I wish I had been awake for it – for all of it – but my body would not allow it. Maybe parts of me did not have the ability to endure it. I fell into my own oblivion and embracing that void got me through the night.

Another morning came.

Nurses came in and gave us their assessment. He would have another day like this. Barbara had to go to work.

I looked at him. He was lying there on his back – his breathing regular, though the inhales were not long and the exhales were little puffs of air, his chest rising and falling with each breath. Regular as clockwork. But the breaths felt like a body that was clinging to life rather than one being nourished by the air he was taking in.

The nurses suggested that I go home and shower, change clothes and come back in an hour. Barbara would stay until I got back and then she would go on to her workday. I was hesitant, but they were reassuring and gave me a pager that attached to my belt and would signal me if anything happened that required me to come back. I headed out of the room telling him that I would be right back.

I walked down to the car, which had transported me to the hospital those many hours ago – it seemed like a different time – a different life. And I began the short drive back to our house.

I knew I should not have left that hospital.

I should not have taken that "break." For years, I was plagued by my agreement to leave, even for such a brief time. I should not have done so. These moments are singular. As Raymond said, "You don't get a second chance." You miss it – you miss it.

No more than ten minutes into my drive, the pager went off. I stopped at one of the three 7-11s that were on the route to our house and used the pay phone to call the number of the phone in the room. Barbara picked up. I asked with urgency, "What's going on?" She was calm but said simply, "Turn around. Come back. Just come back." I hung up. With no vestige of tiredness in me, I urgently drove the ten minutes back to the hospital.

There was a parking spot open, and I grabbed it and ran back into the building and up to his room.

What would I find?

Was he still alive?

Was he gone?

If he is gone, where is his body? I remembered my friend from New York who did not get to see his lover's body.

I raced into the room and stopped. Barbara was standing by his bed. She was calm, quiet, generous, "Jimmy," like my family, she called me Jimmy, "he's gone."

"Gone? But his body is still here!"

And I looked at the bed and yes, his body was still there.

He was dead and I was in the presence of his body.

It was done. Finished. Done.

I was stoic, still, stony. And I looked at Barbara with steel eyes – "What are we supposed to do now?" and she saw me struggling and said softly, "Come over here, Jimmy. Sit with him." And I moved closer to his lifeless body.

And I broke.

I soul-fell into him – the essence of him –

"Oh Raymond! I am so proud of you! You did great! You really did great! I am so proud of you!" And the tears were pouring out of my eyes, and my voice was overly loud, which is my tendency, and I thought a million thoughts – like something I read about people who after they die see the room from above. So, I looked up at the ceiling and imagined him there and started shouting up to the ceiling trying to connect with him. "Goodbye! Goodbye! Raymond! Goodbye! You did great! I am so proud of you! Goodbye!"

I was creating a bit of a scene, and nurses came into the room to get me to calm down or at least to *quiet* down. Hell, I was trying to reach out across the abyss and make sure he heard me. Yeah. Right.

Barbara calmed me down. She said everything was going to be okay.

It was Labor Day weekend. I had to call Ellen, the funeral director. Ellen Rapp. Another angel. In 1990, it wasn't easy to get a funeral home to attend to the corpse of an AIDS patient. I had to call friends in what felt like an AIDS underground. Who do I go to? Invariably, the name of Ellen Rapp was mentioned. She ran a funeral home with its own crematorium in downtown Silver Spring. And she was willing to help people like us. I had stopped-in the week before to take care of all the details. Simple cremation. All arranged and paid for in advance. When the time would come, it was simply a matter of flipping the switch to "go."

Now, at this moment, all I could do was sit and stare at any available floor. We started to move to the door of the hospital room, and I looked back over my shoulder and turned to take in his lifeless body one more time. His eyes were half open, with a blank stare that assured me that no one was there. If he was anywhere, he was certainly not there. I wasn't ready to leave. I moved back to him, wanting some little gesture – nice, calm, memorable – that I could take with me. Something beautiful. I tried to close his eyes. Like in the movies.

The result wasn't what I intended. Closing his eyelids made his face droop oddly. He didn't even look like himself. I thought, "What have I done?" I used my fingers to adjust his eyes, molding them as best I could. In a matter of seconds, I managed to get him to look more like himself. This farcical moment was the perfect end to a story that often felt like one big and long and cruel joke.

But this was no joke. A life was over. They said I would be OK. I was about to walk through a doorway, which would, whether I wanted it or not, be the portal to a new chapter in my life.

I wanted time to stop.

I did not want to go through that door. I did not want to separate myself from the person I had lost. I wanted everything to freeze – just for a day, an hour, a minute. A moment?

But time does not do that. It does not freeze.

I was *not* OK. I walked through that door into an unknown beginning. I was not OK. I resented it. I did not want it. Quite simply, I hated it. And I was not OK at all.

EPILOGUE

Back in April it was, before the PML took over, before his dementia, before the beginning of the final exit – I dared to imagine the year's end and opened a conversation with him about what we might do to celebrate another year passing – another victory on the longevity train. And he got quiet. I asked him if anything was wrong.

"James. Don't be upset with me. But I don't think I have another Christmas in me. I'm exhausted. I just can't keep this up. Don't be upset with me. I'm sorry. I will be OK. It's *you* I'm worried about. You are going to be a mess."

Our roles reversed at that moment. I became the patient and he became my caregiver. Just for that moment. He told me that he wanted me to thank everyone for him, and I told him that I could do that and that I would do that. And he said thank you, softly. Thank you.

Here I am, on the other side of it all. And there is nothing. I live in my own oblivion. Willfully. Thinking, "Make it all just stop!"

Our funeral director, Ellen, had given me a share of his ashes. It was "between us" because the family dynamic between his parent and me was toxic. Ellen gave them to me in a small wooden box. She told me it was small because this was the kind of box that was used for the ashes of infants and babies. Inside, it housed the fragments of crushed bone that were the only tangible parts of him left me. Stuffed into the little box. The bone fragments lived in a little baggie.

I put the little box on the little mantle of the fake fireplace in our little house. I surrounded it with some of his most prized trinkets. Yeah, it was a little bit of a shrine. I needed a place to simply stand and stare.

I really wanted to disappear, but my good people at work asked me to delay my much-needed time away until a project was done.

One Saturday morning, I was at the theatre. When I got home in the afternoon, I found the door of the house ajar. I hurried in and sure enough, the place had been ransacked. Stereo components – gone. VCR – gone. Drawers were askew and cabinets hung open. Upstairs, my box of important papers – birth certificate, social security card, passport – gone. I was suddenly gripped with a thought and raced down to the fake fireplace in the living room to discover that he was gone, too.

They had taken the fragments of my dead love.

They had taken the box, the baggie, and the bones.

Those fuckers!

I sat down on the floor surrounded by the debris of theft and stared into the rug. My one thought, "I guess we don't get to hold onto anything in life. It all goes. The only thing you get to hold onto, at least for a while, is yourself. And the fragments of thought inside your head."

After a few days, the phone rang. I let the machine answer – I usually screened my calls. I heard the voice say, "Hello Jim. This is Ellen Rapp . . . " and I bolted toward the phone, picked up the receiver, and said, "Yes! Ellen! It's Jim – I'm here."

She asked, "Jim, where's Raymond?" and I told her the story, wondering what she might know. The break-in, the missing box and ashes. She said, "Well, I got this phone call from people in your neighborhood. They saw my business label on the bottom of the box and called to tell me they had it. They said their grandson found it in the backyard. You can go pick it up anytime."

I was delighted! "Thank you, Ellen! I will let you know what happens!"

I took the address and walked up the street to the house. I knocked on the door and an elderly couple answered together. They seemed extremely nervous and I told them who I was and that Ellen had called me and how grateful I was. I did everything I could to put them at ease. They handed me the box with a paper towel over it. I removed the paper towel and opened it up and was devastated to find it empty. I asked about the contents. Had they seen a baggie? Or any white crumbly material? They said they had not and that their grandson was a good boy and would not keep that away from them if he had it.

My Spidey sense went off, and I thought that the grandson may have been more involved than I had originally thought. No matter. Rather than make accusations, I said, "Thank you for the box and for calling Ellen. If, by any chance you do come across that baggie, please put it in my mailbox." I pointed to my house down the street. I told them, slowly and deliberately, that there would be no questions and nothing but appreciation. With that, I said goodbye and walked home carrying my empty box.

A few days later, I went to check the mail. Lo and behold, there was the baggie – in the mailbox. A little less volume than before his trip, but he was there and I took him into the house and restored the baggie to its home in the little wooden box. I said, "Welcome back. I hope you had a good vacation." And felt some peace that he had found his way home to me. He always found his way home.

Time passed. The world moved forward. But I didn't.

I was still stuck on the day he left.

September 1, 1990.

I was not prepared.

I was not relieved.

I was not at peace.

I wobbled between lostness and anger.

I wasn't angry at anyone in particular – just angry.

And then lost.

And then – numb.

"Shouldn't the world stop? He stopped. I stopped."

But everything around me kept going, absorbing his absence while poking at my pain.

Everything transforms into a new reality. "Life goes on," they say.

Must it?

I wanted everything to stop, even though I knew that was an absurd desire.

"Just stop – damn you all!"

"I'm sorry for your loss." God, I hated that phrase.

And you hear it all the time. It's meant to be comforting!

"I'm sorry for your loss." My loss? Fuck that!

He is gone! We all lose because he is gone. You lose We *all* lose! Of course, I lose, but *you* lose, too! *We all fucking lose*!

The day of the memorial service came. September 13, 1990. Unity Church on Capitol Hill. He had sung in their choir, had enjoyed the friendships he made there, and had found a community that liked him – even loved him as one of their own. They had become our extended family through those last years. And they came out in force for his memorial, along with the many friends and creative comrades from the theatre community that had always embraced him and us.

Here was a gathering that acknowledged our collective loss of him. His loss was all our loss. Finally, the world stopped for a moment to pay attention to him. Only him, which he so deserved. Per his instructions, I thanked the many – each by name and action. The many who had walked with us during all or part of the long five and a half years that had begun on a weekday morning when he awakened me with a persistent cough in late January of 1985. How long ago. How naïve we were. How far away.

I finally got my blessed two weeks away from work.

I saw no one.

I read many books about life and its meaning – or the search for its meaning and its mysteries. I steeped myself in words. At night I would sleep on the rug on the floor of the living room, still not daring to sleep upstairs in the bedroom. I resisted any return to normalcy.

One evening came and my good friend Jim – yes, another Jim – was at the door and he said that he wanted to take me out. He insisted that I needed to get out of the house and that he had planned a night of bar hopping to all the D.C. gay bars and clubs. I looked at him like he was crazy and said, "Jim, that's about the last thing I want to do right now." He said that was why it had to be done and that he wasn't going to accept my refusal. After a quick but careful review of my closet, he made me put on a particular shirt and a particular pair of jeans, saying "that should do" and packed me up into his red pick-up truck.

He always had a way of making me laugh – I can't say I didn't have a fun time with him that night. We went to Remington's, the country/western bar, the show tune piano bar, the collegiate bar, and lastly, the leather bar.

I had only been to the D.C. Eagle once in my life. Before going in, I protested that it was late and that I didn't have the capacity to do another bar and another drink. But he wouldn't hear of it and in we went.

The place was packed and the cigarette smoke hung dense, which I like. The music was loud and it was a big party. I wandered around the place, losing Jim in the crowd. When I found him, he was lost in conversation. I gathered it would be best to leave him to it.

I walked up to the front bar, where a young man was bartending – actually, he was holding court with an enthusiastic crowd that was hanging out at what was clearly "his" bar. He asked me if I needed anything and I responded with the obligatory request for an Amstel Light. He got it to me fast and I handed him a ten-dollar bill. He brought me the change. I reached out my hand, palm up to receive it. He looked directly into my eyes as he took my hand from beneath; with his other hand, he placed the bills into my palm and slowly dragged his hand over mine.

Well.

This was clearly a rehearsed and practiced and, dare I say, highly effective move.

I looked at him – closely – into his eyes. He took the challenge and held his look back into mine.

I saw a glimmer there that made me smile the kind of radiant smile that comes when you are living life – not merely marking time – the kind of smile that despite yourself has you engaged in the world and the people in it. I put two dollars on the bar as a tip.

He smiled and without hurry said, "Thanks! I'm Jamie."

And I said, "Hi, Jamie. I'm Jim."

ABOUT THE AUTHOR

Jim Petosa is Professor Emeritus at Boston University's College of Fine Arts, where he served as Director of the School of Theatre (2002-2019) and continued as member of the faculty through 2023. He served as artistic director of Greater Boston's New Repertory Theatre (2012-2018), Boston Center for American Performance (2009-2019), and Olney Theatre Center in the DC area from 1994-2011. He is co-artistic director of Potomac Theatre Project/PTP/NYC (1987-present). He has directed plays, operas, and musicals throughout his long career. As a guest director, he has worked at the Smithsonian Institution, Wolf Trap Farm Park, The Kennedy Center for the Performing Arts, D.C.'s Studio Theatre, RoundHouse Theatre, and many others. As a spoken word actor, he has worked with the National Philharmonic Orchestra at Strathmore Hall, the Boston University Orchestra, Eclipse Chamber Orchestra, New Collage Music for which he recorded Donald Sur's THE LADY AND THE UNICORN, conducted by David Hoose. He has taught at The Catholic University of America, which is his alma mater, University of Maryland at College Park, George Washington University, Georgetown University, and Middlebury College among others. He is the recipient of the Helen Hayes Award for Outstanding Director of a Musical (JACQUES BREL IS ALIVE AND WELL), and a nominee for Outstanding Director of a Play (COLLECTED STORIES) and the Charles MacArthur Award for Outstanding New Play for his collaboration with Carole Graham Lehan on the biographically inspired LOOK! WE HAVE COME THROUGH! about the lives and marriage of D.H. and Frieda Lawrence.

A member of Actor's Equity and the Society of Directors and Choreographers for which he has served as a member of the Executive Board, Petosa is a current board member and past president of Becket Arts Center, chair of the City of Quincy's LGBTQ+ Commission, and has served on the Board of Governors at United First Parish Church in Quincy, MA.

www.ingramcontent.com/pod-product-compliance
Lightning Source LLC
LaVergne TN
LVHW051012080826
845145LV00009B/2589

* 9 7 8 1 9 6 8 9 1 9 3 7 5 *